Stories from the countryside

Of India

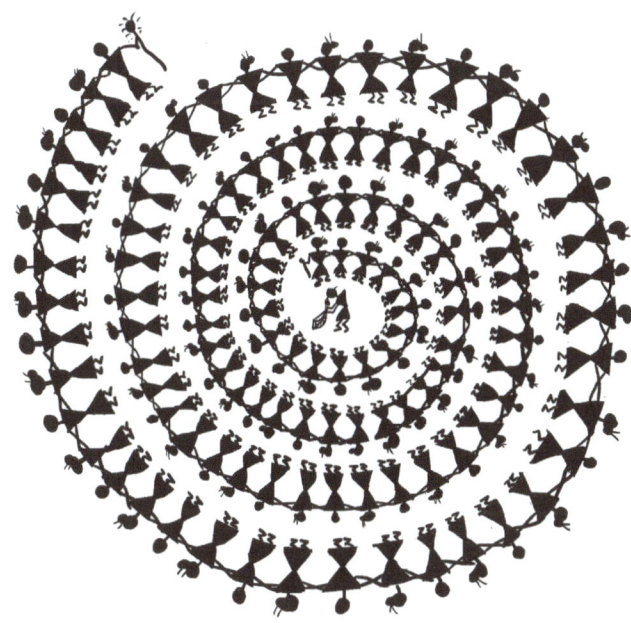

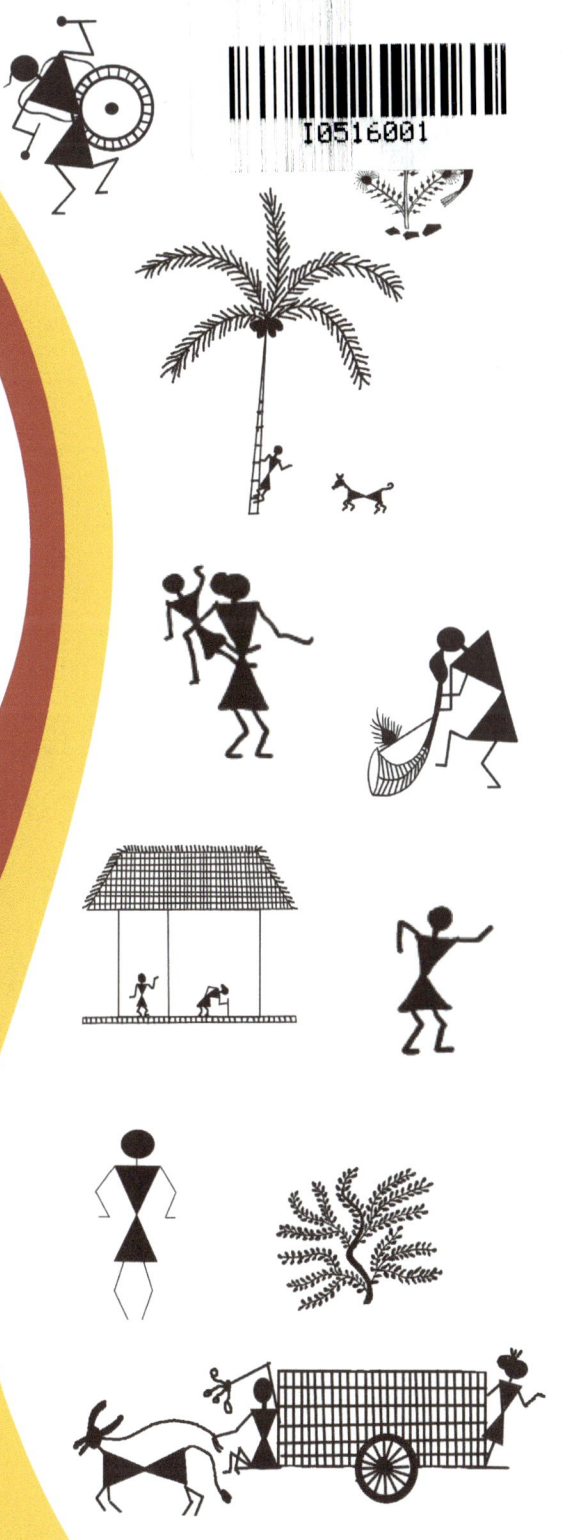

Story and Warli illustration

Namitha Tantri

ISBN: 9798394084775
Independently published
Copyright©2023 Namitha Tantri
All rights reserved

For all countryside and Warli art lovers

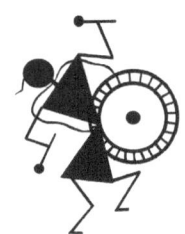 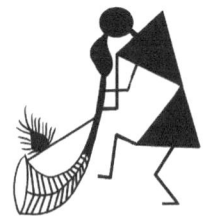

What is Warli art?

Warli art is an ancient form of tribal art that originates from the Warli tribe in the western state of Maharashtra, India. It is one of the oldest folk art forms in the region. The art is characterized by simple, yet expressive, geometric shapes and patterns that depict daily life, nature, and rituals.

Warli art is known for its distinctive style, featuring simple geometric shapes such as circles, triangles, and squares. The figures are painted using white pigment made from a mixture of rice paste and water on a dark background, typically made from mud. The art predominantly depicts scenes from tribal life, showcasing daily activities, celebrations, rituals, and nature. The human figures are represented in basic shapes, often in groups, engaged in various activities like dancing, farming, hunting, and ceremonies.

Warli art is deeply rooted in the tribal rituals and traditions of the Warli community. It is often used during weddings, harvest festivals, and other important ceremonies to decorate walls and floors as a way of invoking blessings and ensuring prosperity. Warli art is traditionally a communal activity, where groups of women come together to create artwork. They sing, dance, and paint the walls of houses or the floor for special occasions, fostering a sense of unity and cultural preservation within the community.

The Author, Namitha Tantri, has used Warli art to illustrate the story in this book. The stories within the book are fictional, inspired by the author's cherished childhood memories, and do not represent any specific community or people.

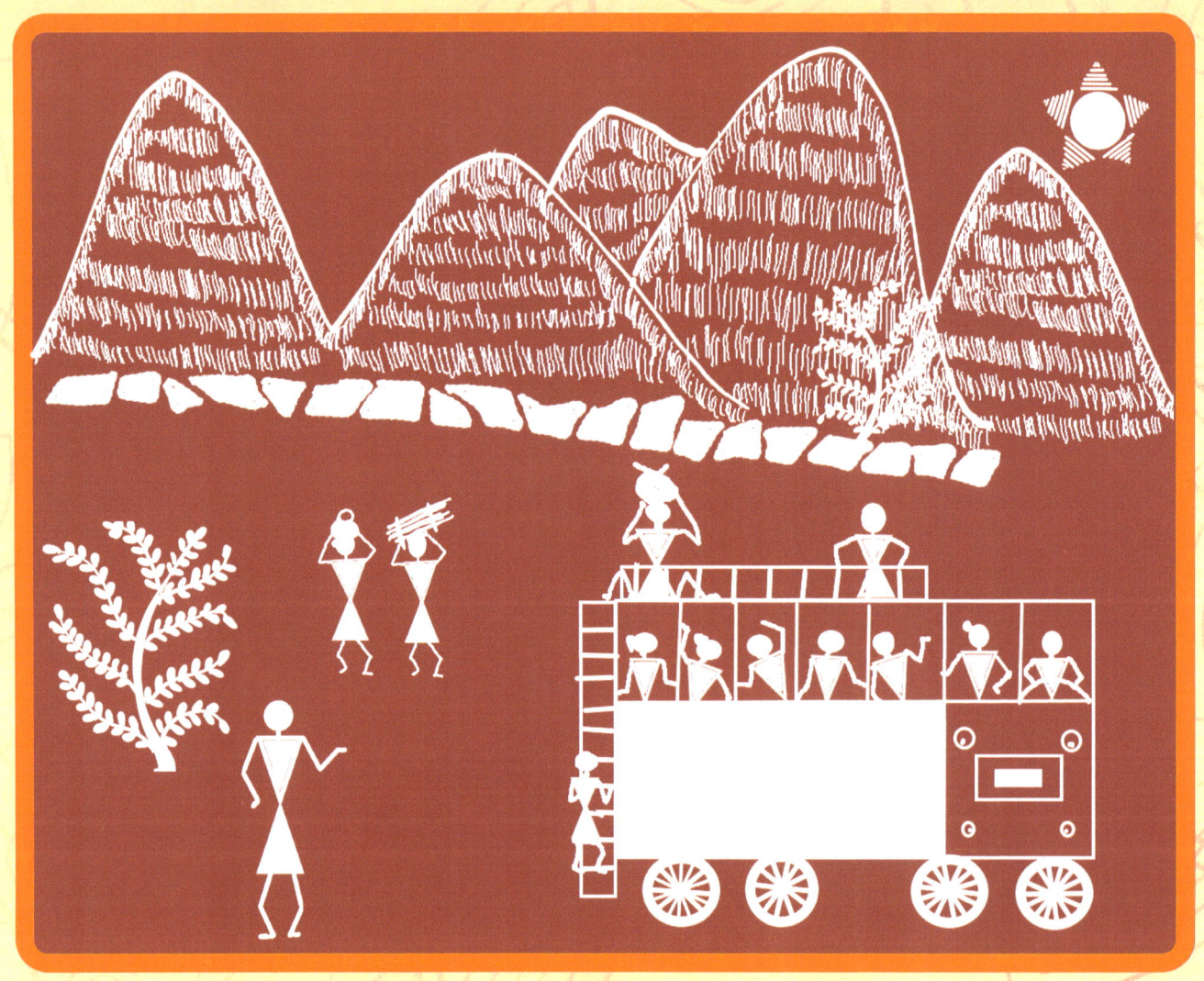

I will share with you,
stories from the **countryside**
making sure a part of
your land story will also coincide!

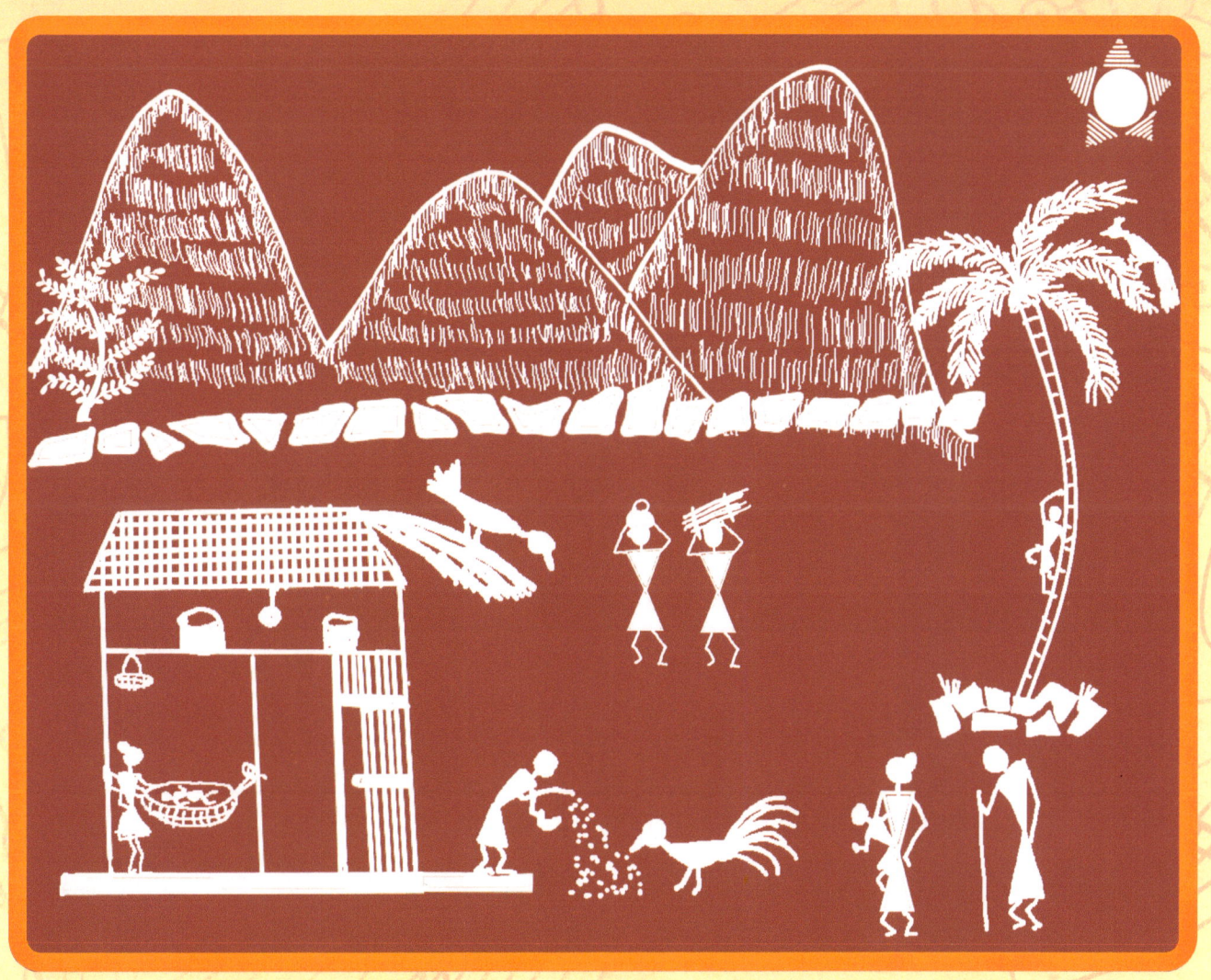

The land makes you feel
that you are part of a miracle,
and from **people**, you learn that
simplicity is a way to move forward!

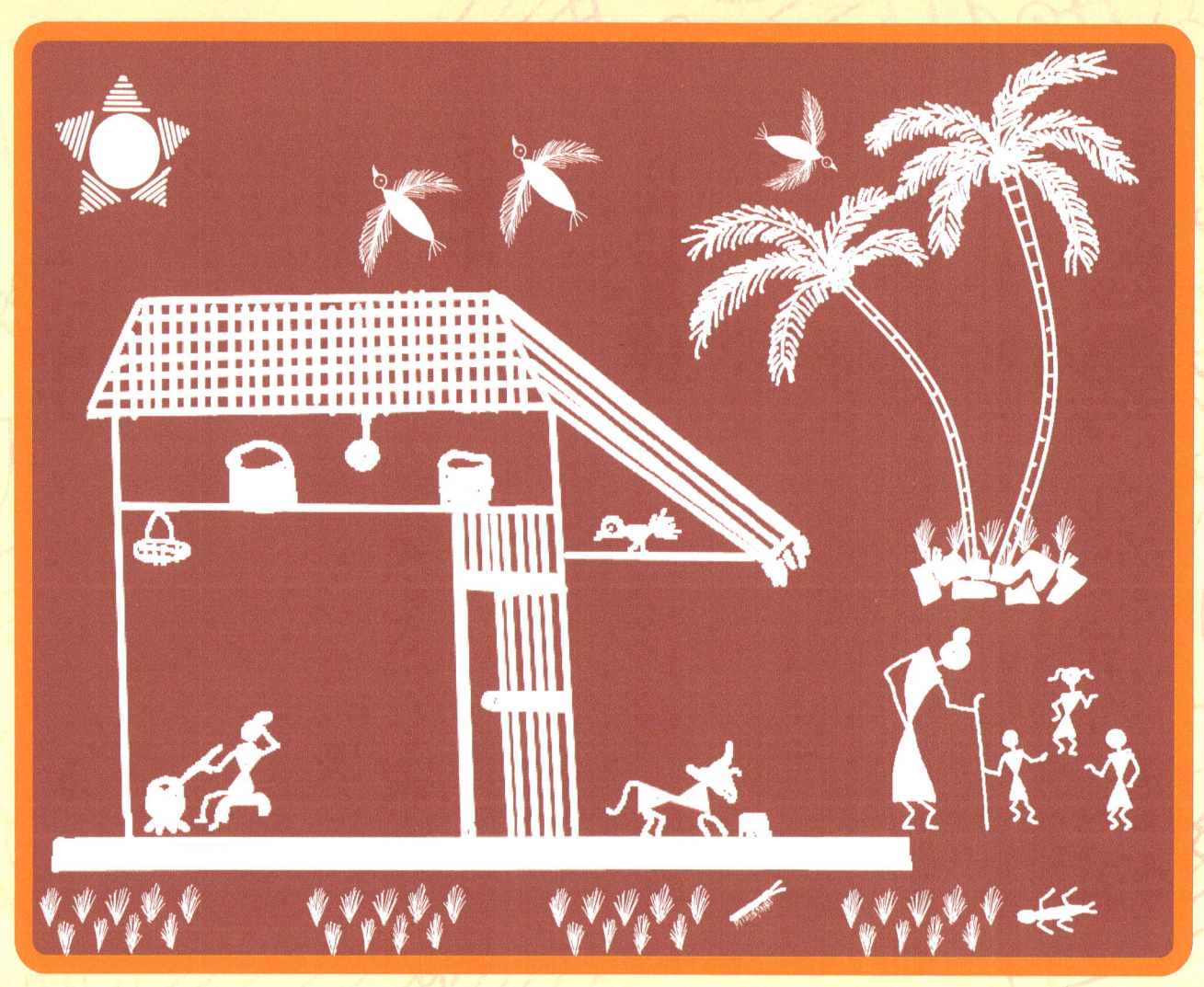

We live in a **Hut**
with walls covered with mud.
You can find no windows
and doors that are never shut.

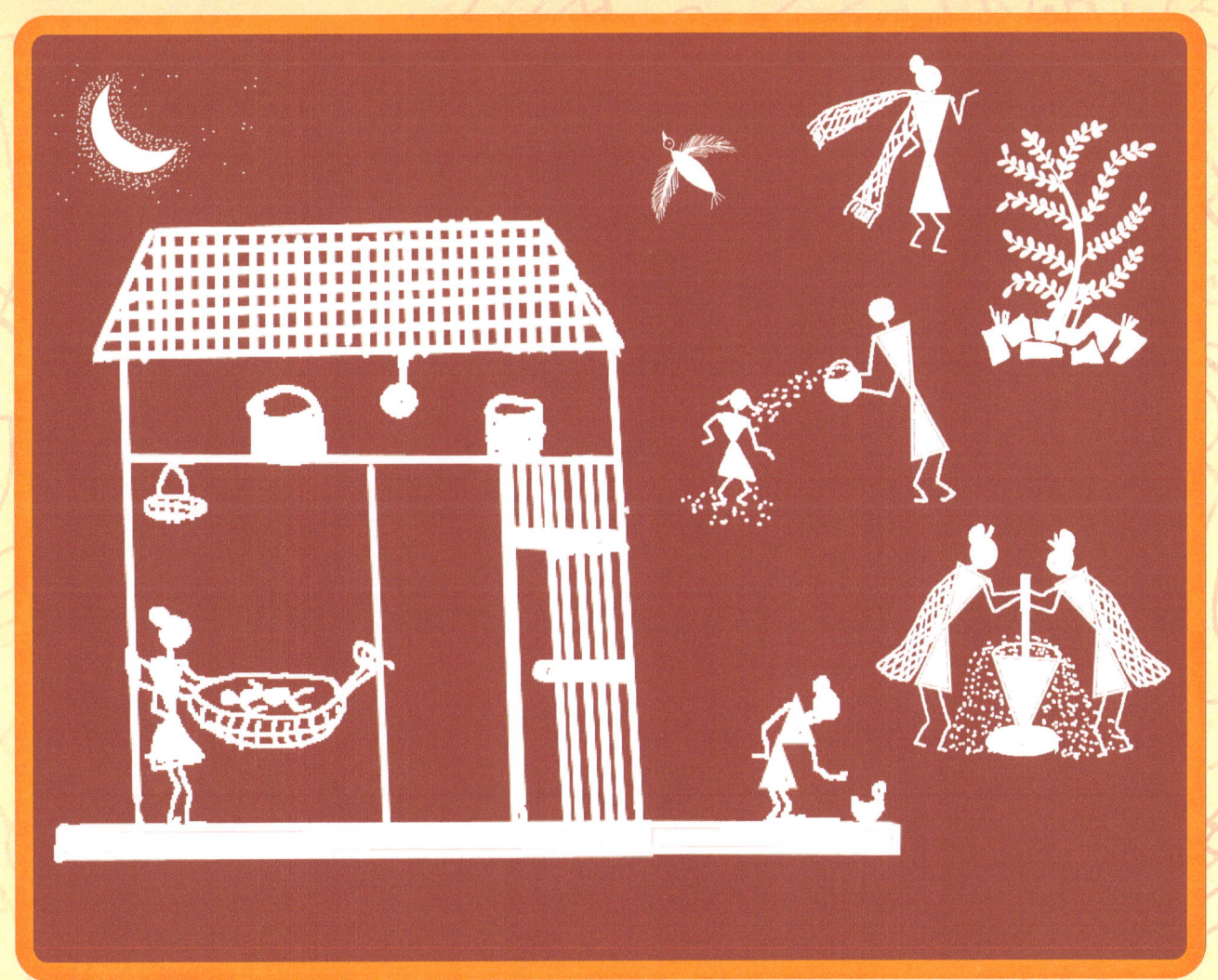

Mother brightens the darkest night
Even when things are just not right.
She makes sure that we are all united,
we stayed together and never separated.

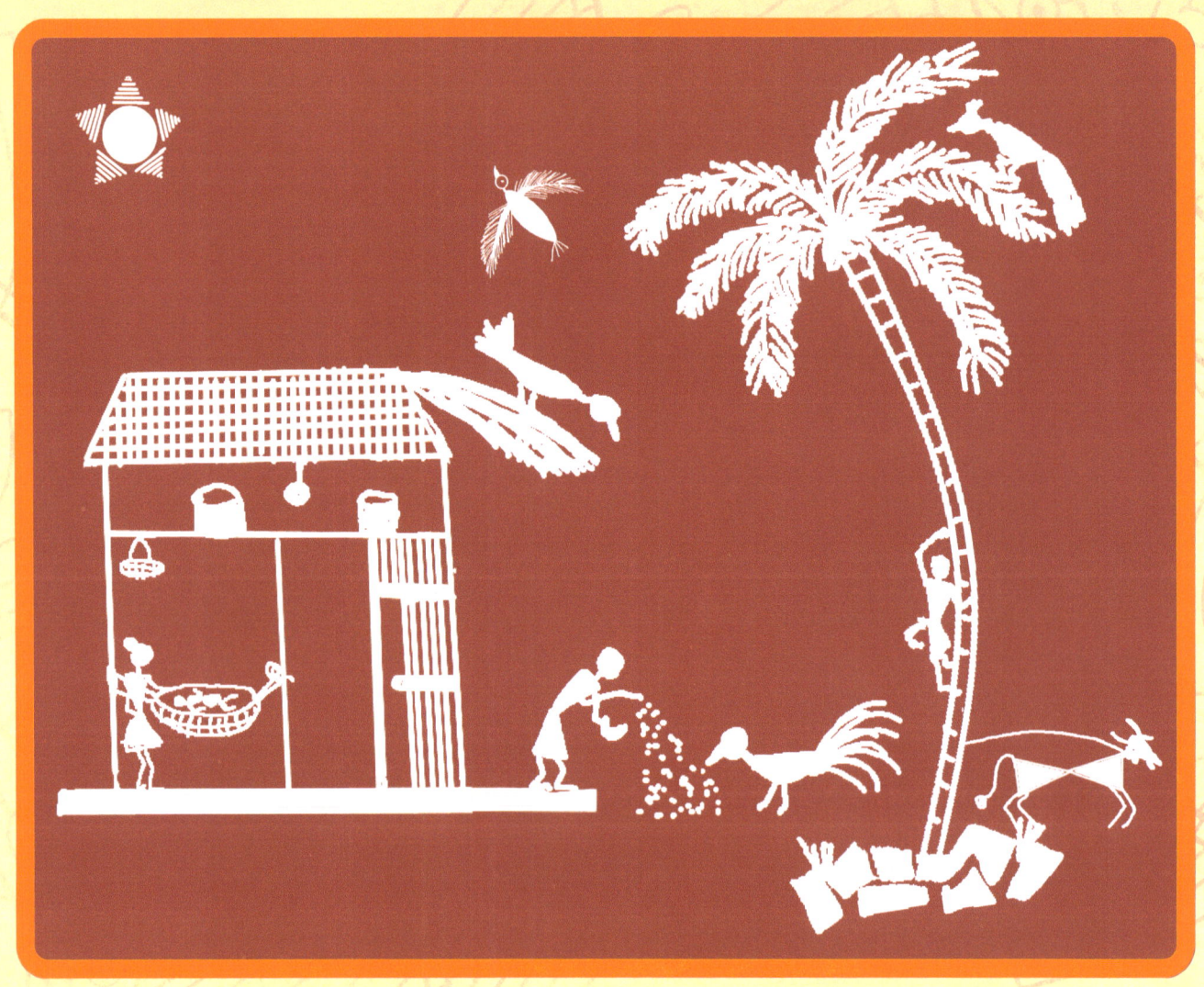

Every morning comes a **bird**
singing the melody ever unheard
we feed the birds with love and care
and try not to scare them away.

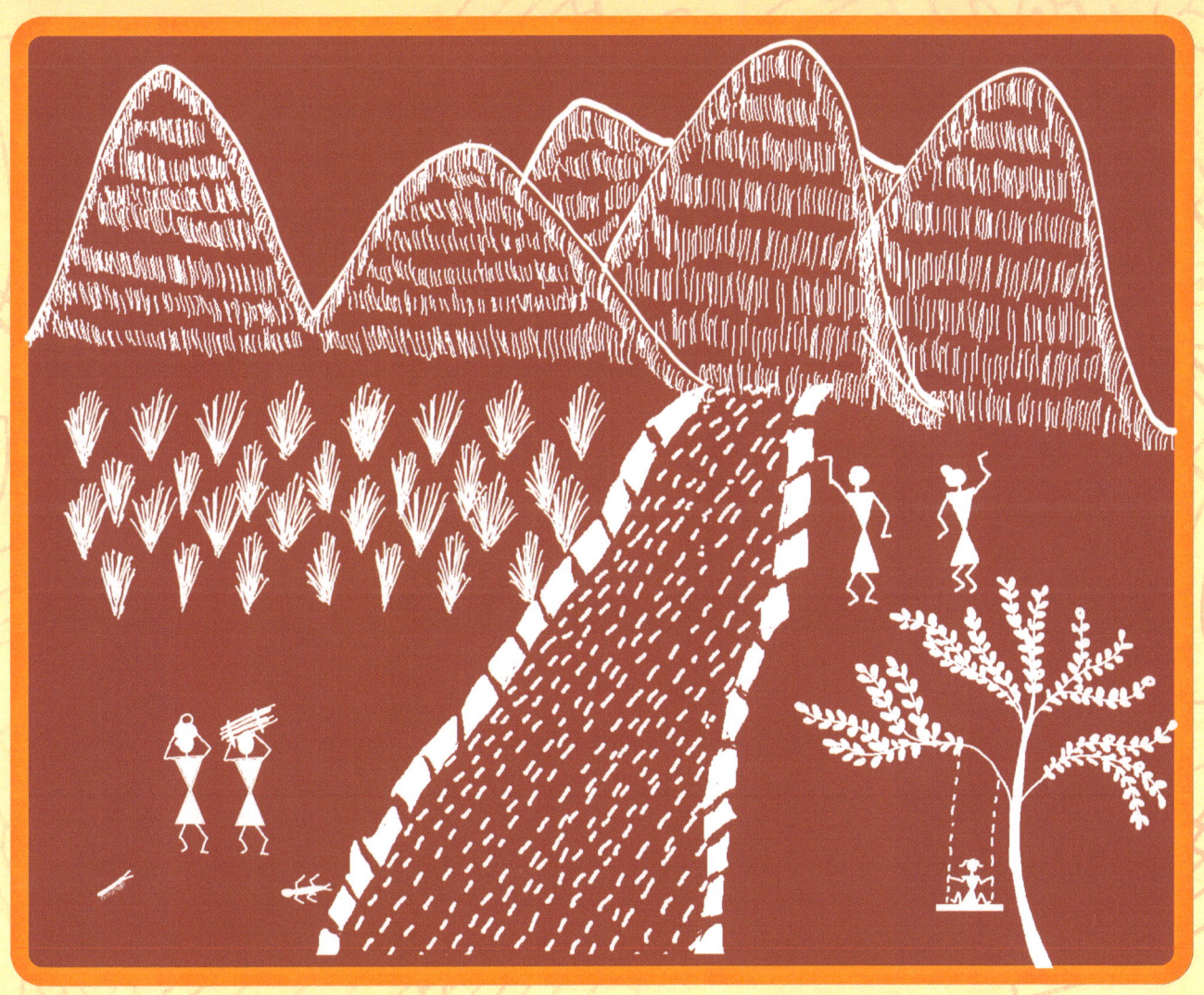

When we are bored for awhile
we go on **nature trails** nearby.
It is a track with a view
of mountains and rivers flowing through.

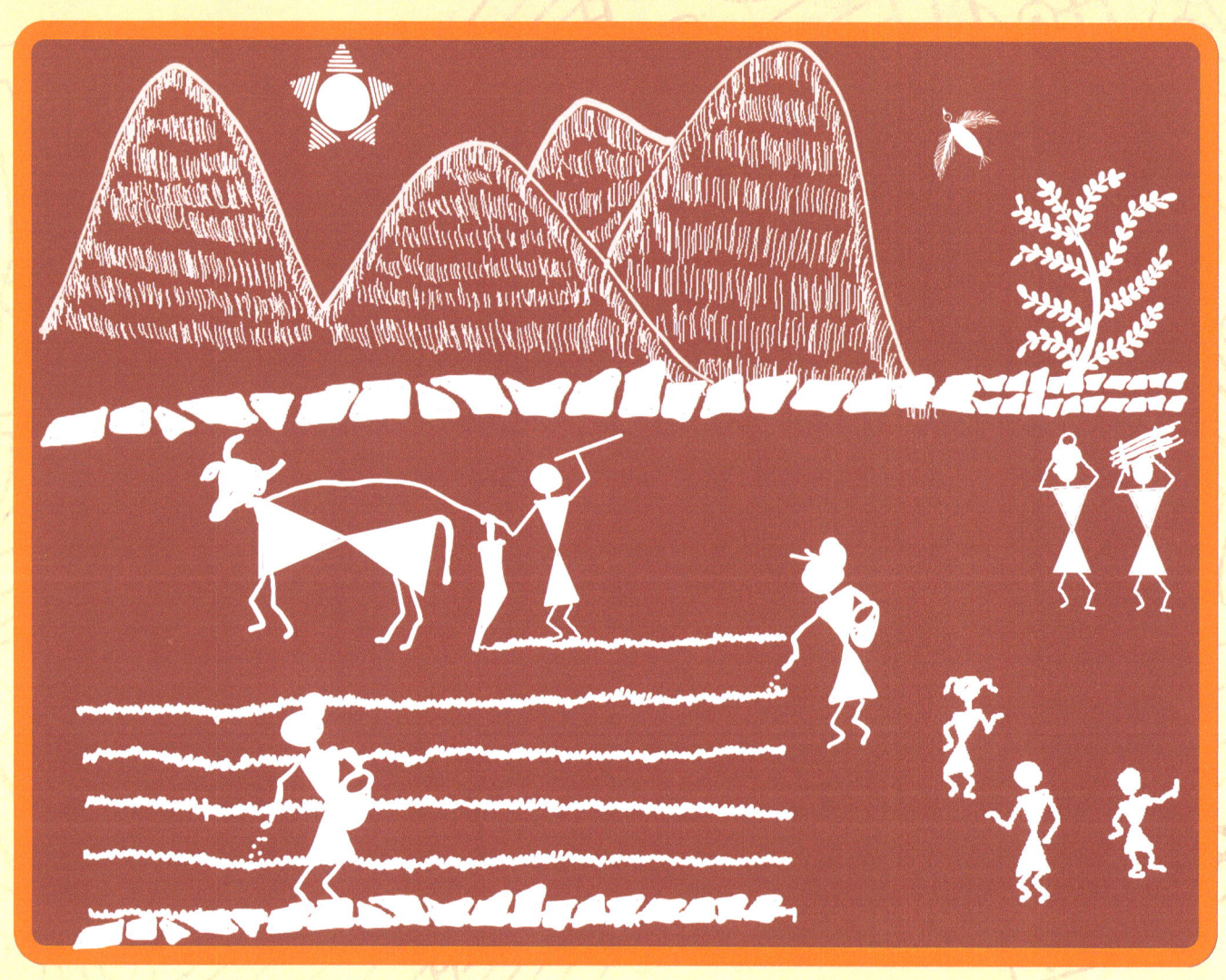

We sow the crop seed
in our beautiful **field**,
That guarantees us a fortune
when in need!

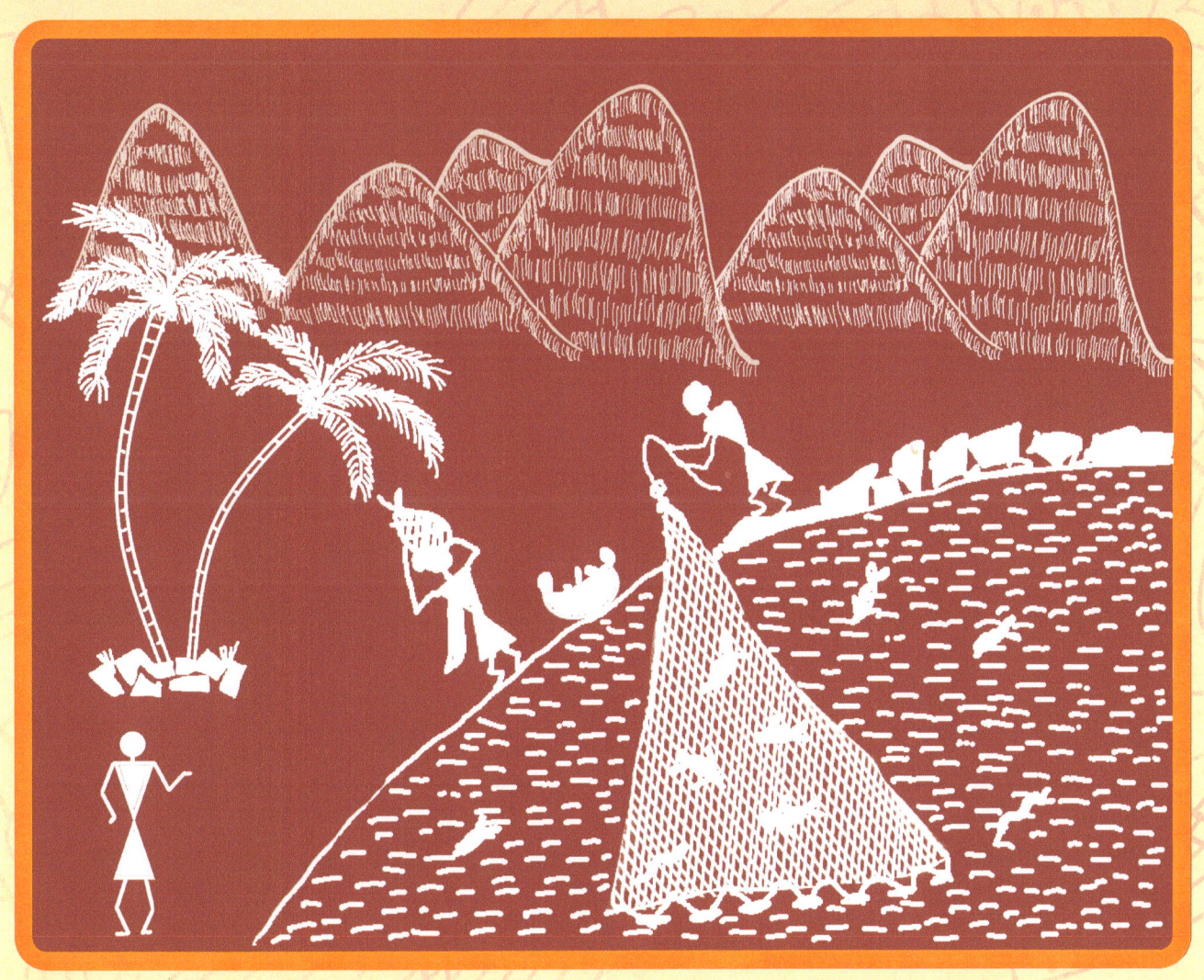

I am still learning
the art of **Fishing**
for you know
It's a skill needed for our living!

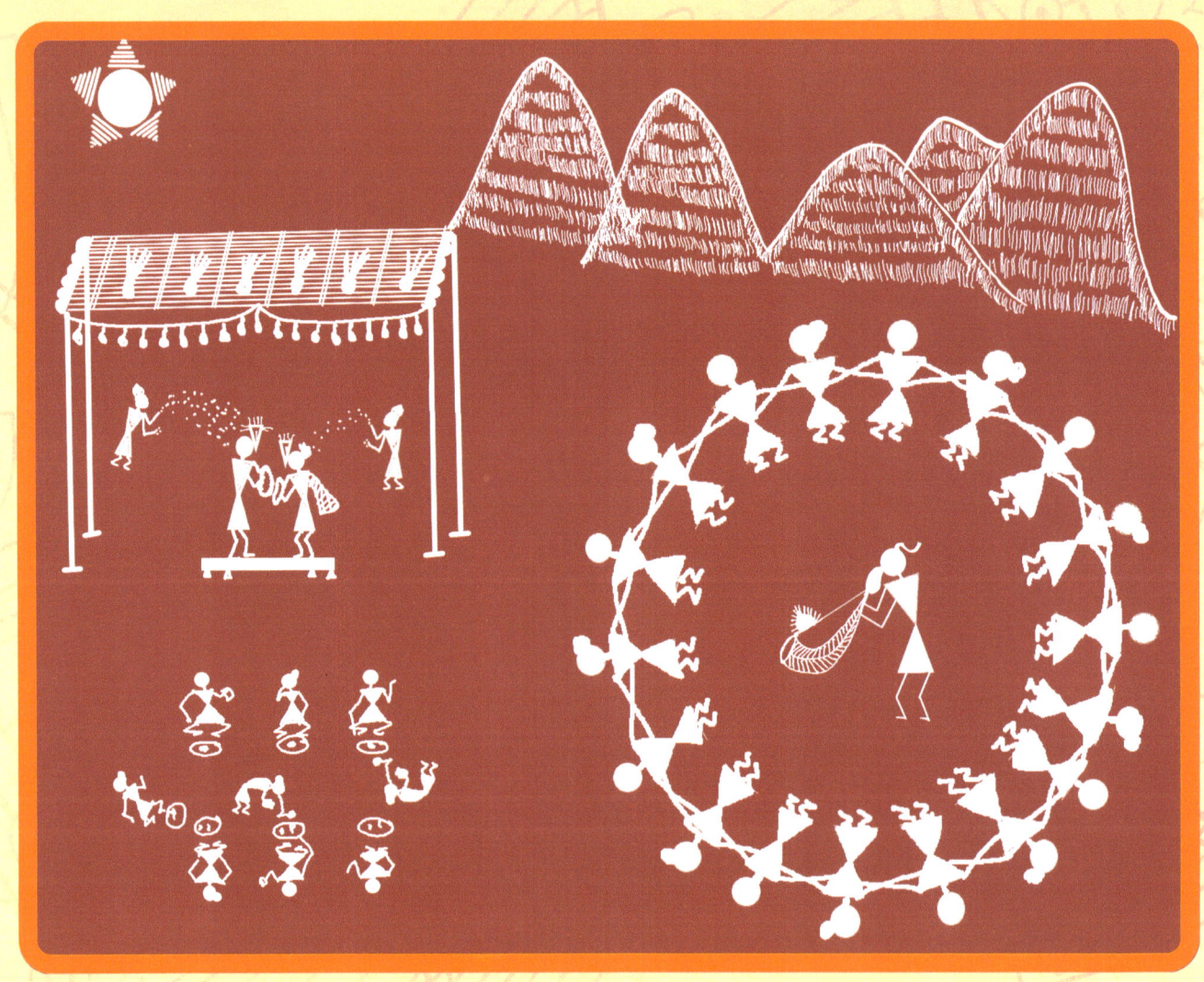

Dancing together
gives us pleasure.
To spread the happiness
that we all treasure.

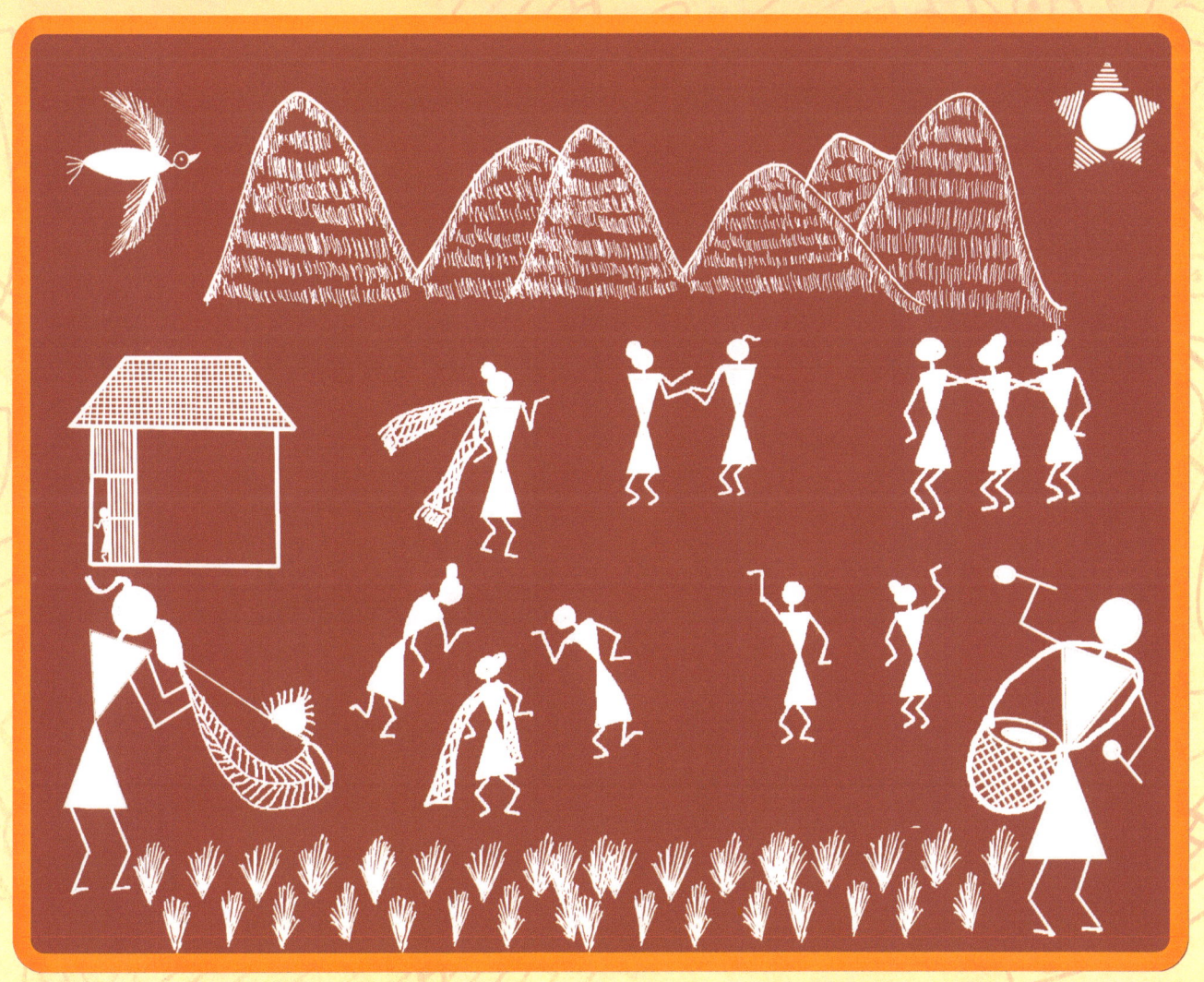

When we play **Tarpa** and **drum**,
you will surely come
To dance to the beats
On your happy feet.

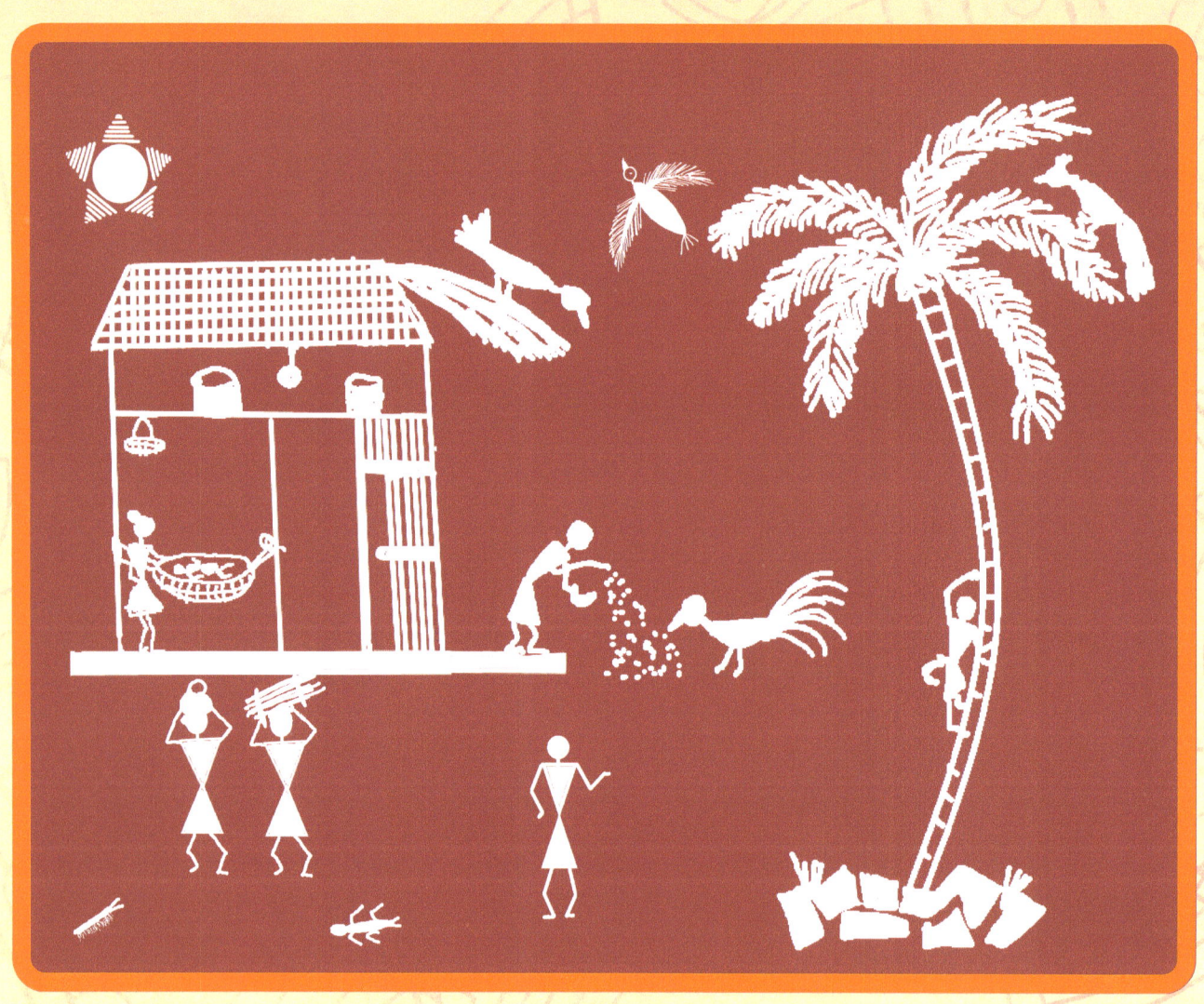

Insects crawling around,
Or a bird building a nest
We find everything amusing
and conserve them as our belonging.

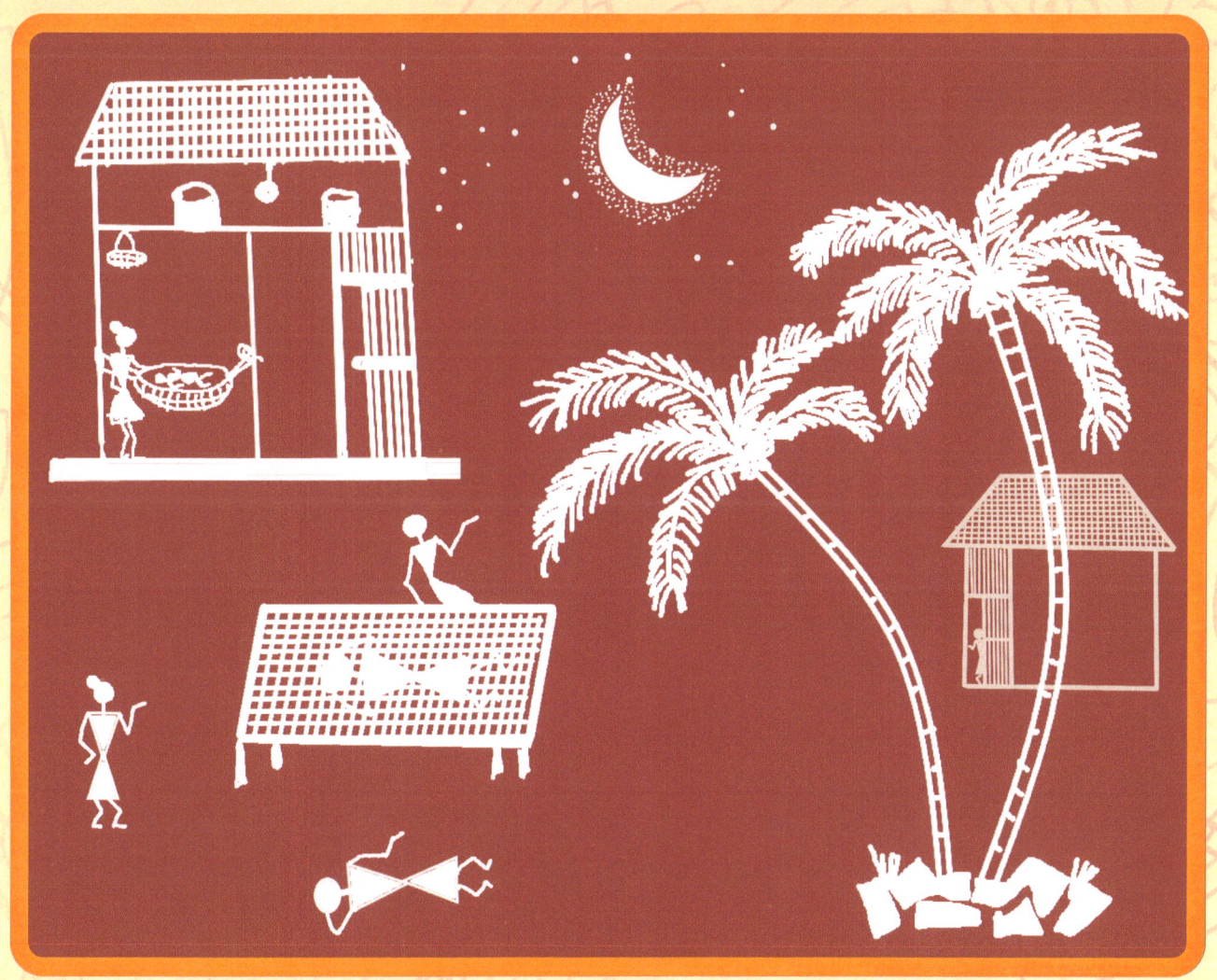

The stars that shine so bright
the moon that conquers the **night**
grateful to every other miracle
that makes us think everything is all right!

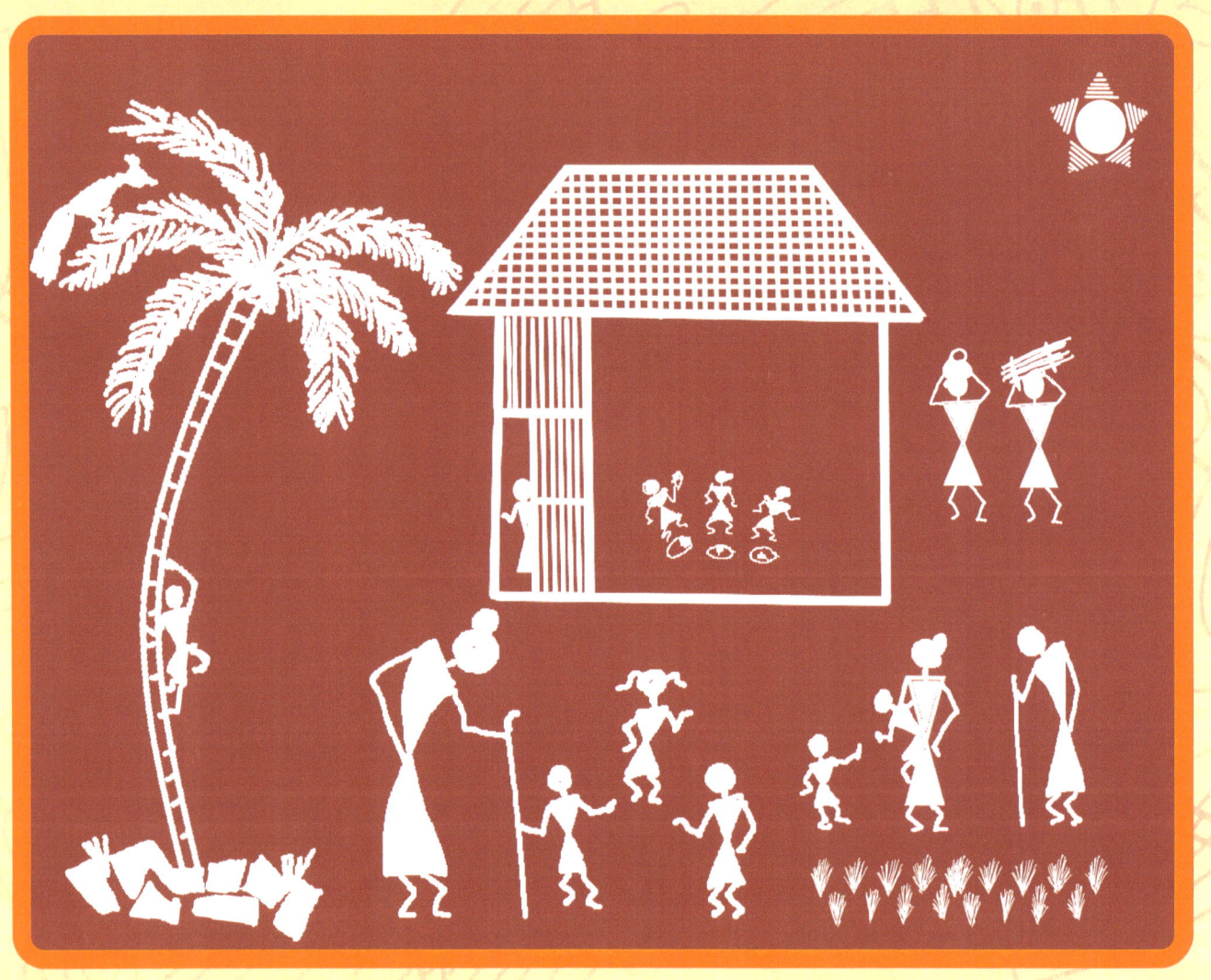

My **Grandma** Is the best
She puts all our doubts to rest
She shares her wisdom through her stories
relieving all our worries.

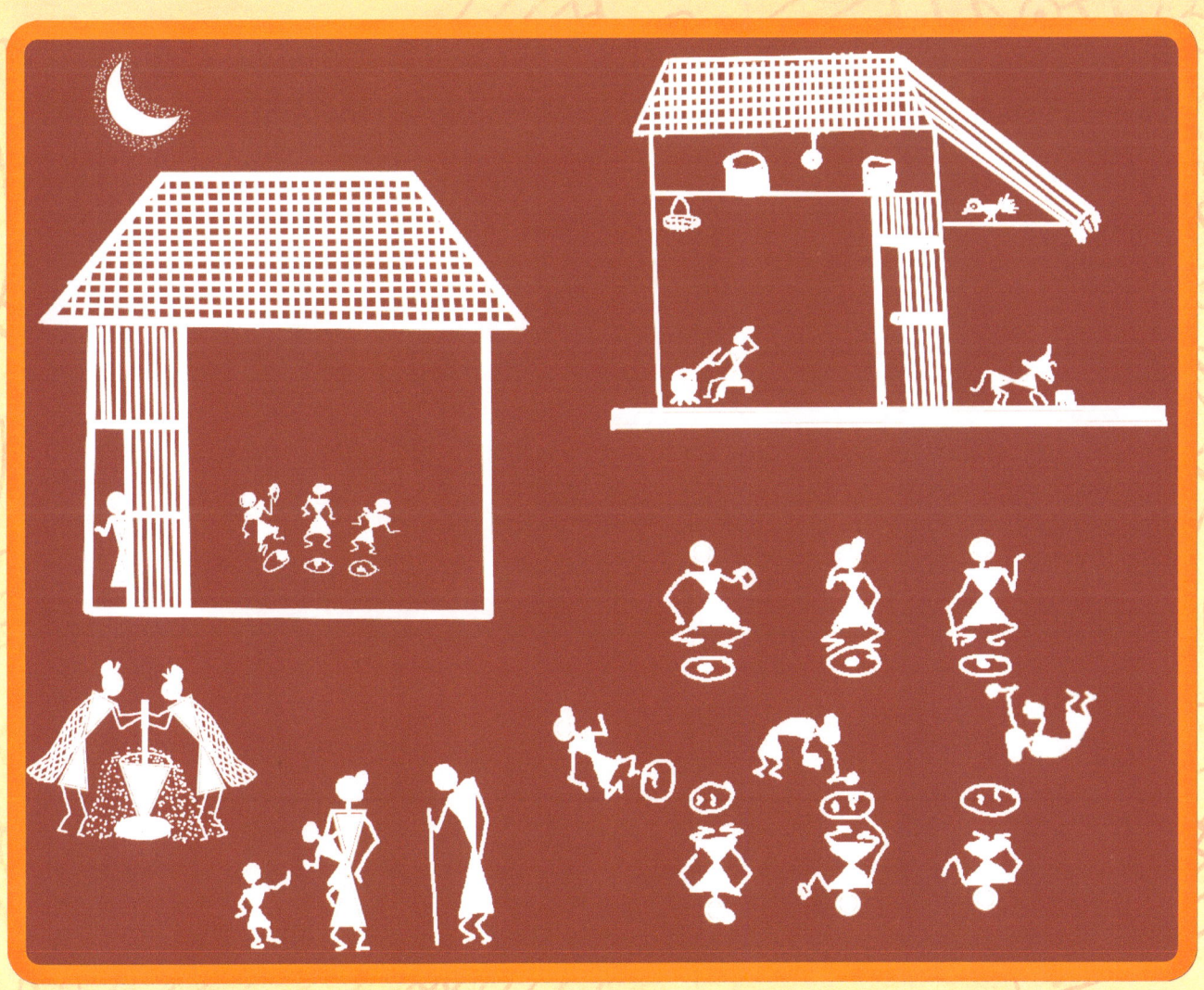

We make sure
to have our **meals** together
for that gives us a chance
to know each other much better.

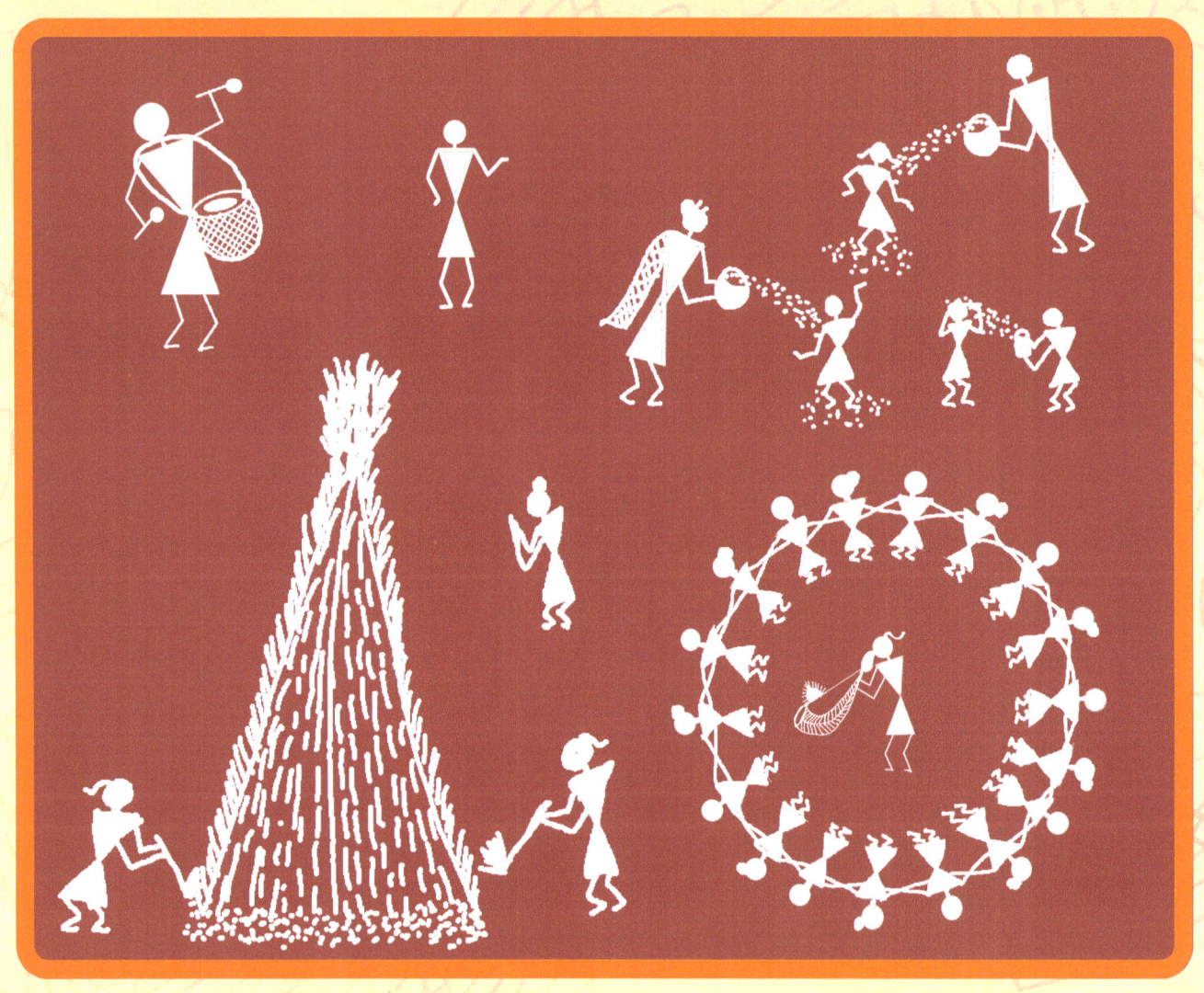

Of all the holy rituals, **Holi** is the best,
where people gather together
around the bonfire at night
and splash coloured water when bright.

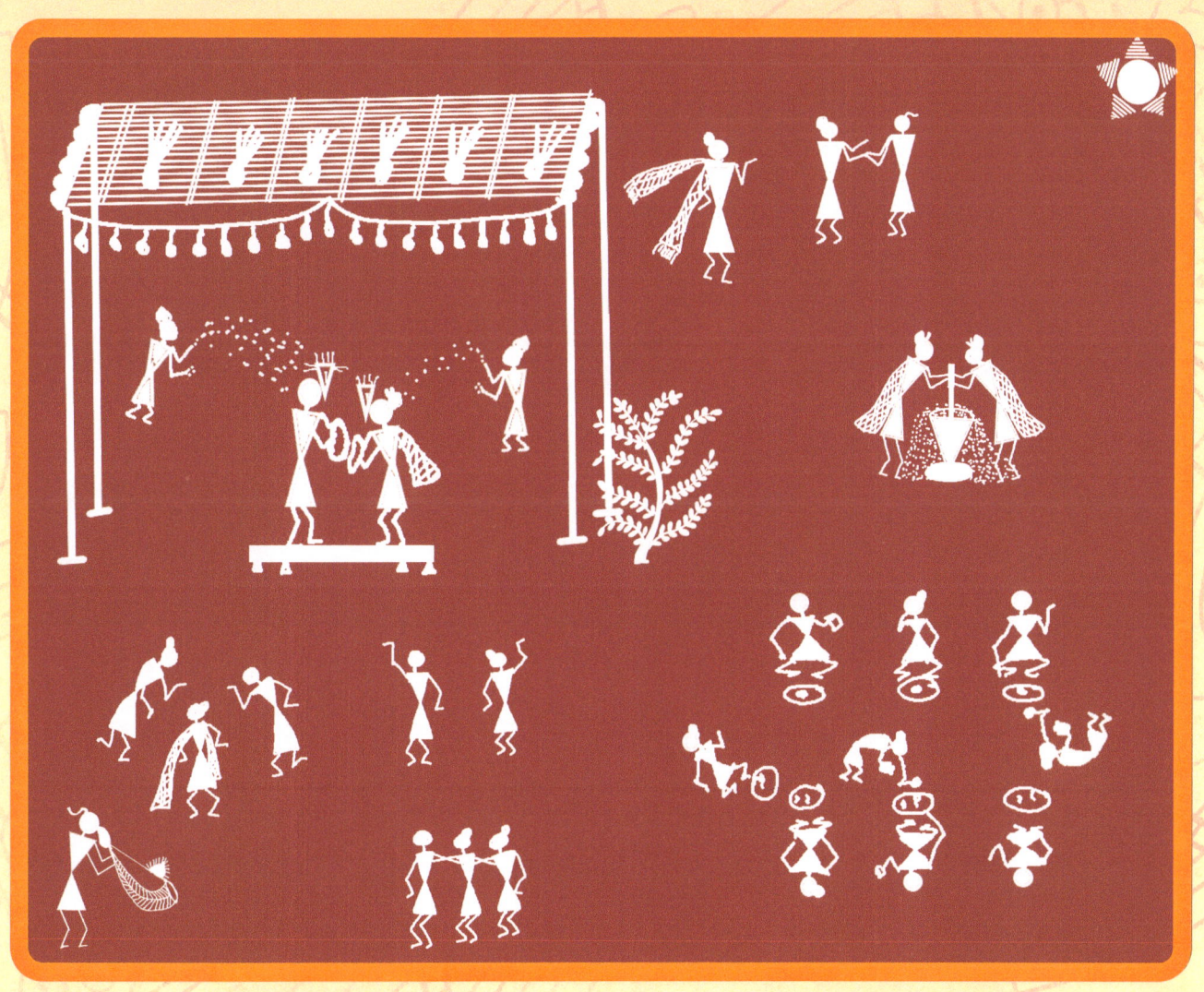

You will learn more about our culture
when you attend
a countryside **wedding** for sure.

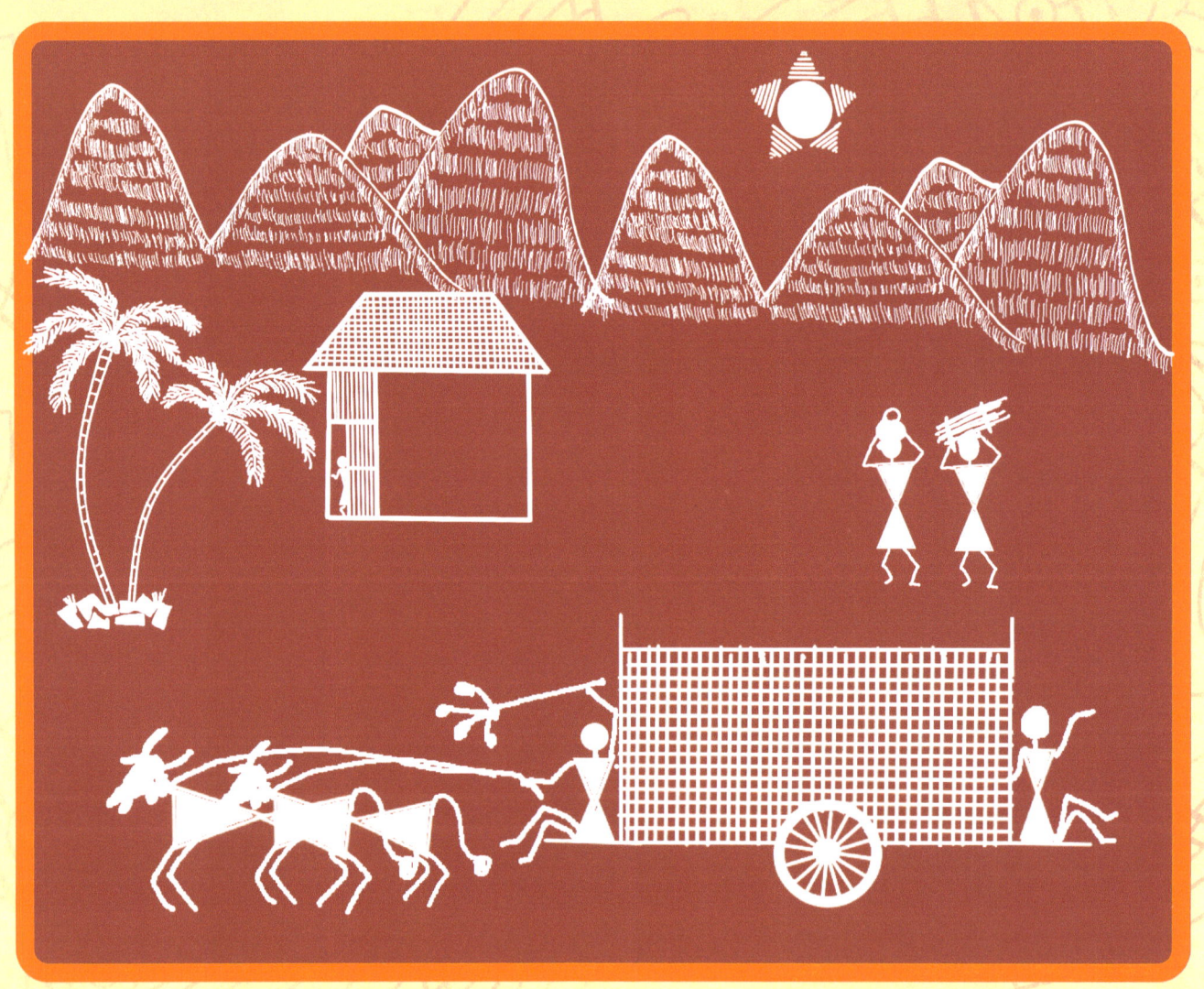

We like to travel in **Bullock** cart
with friendly bulls tied apart.

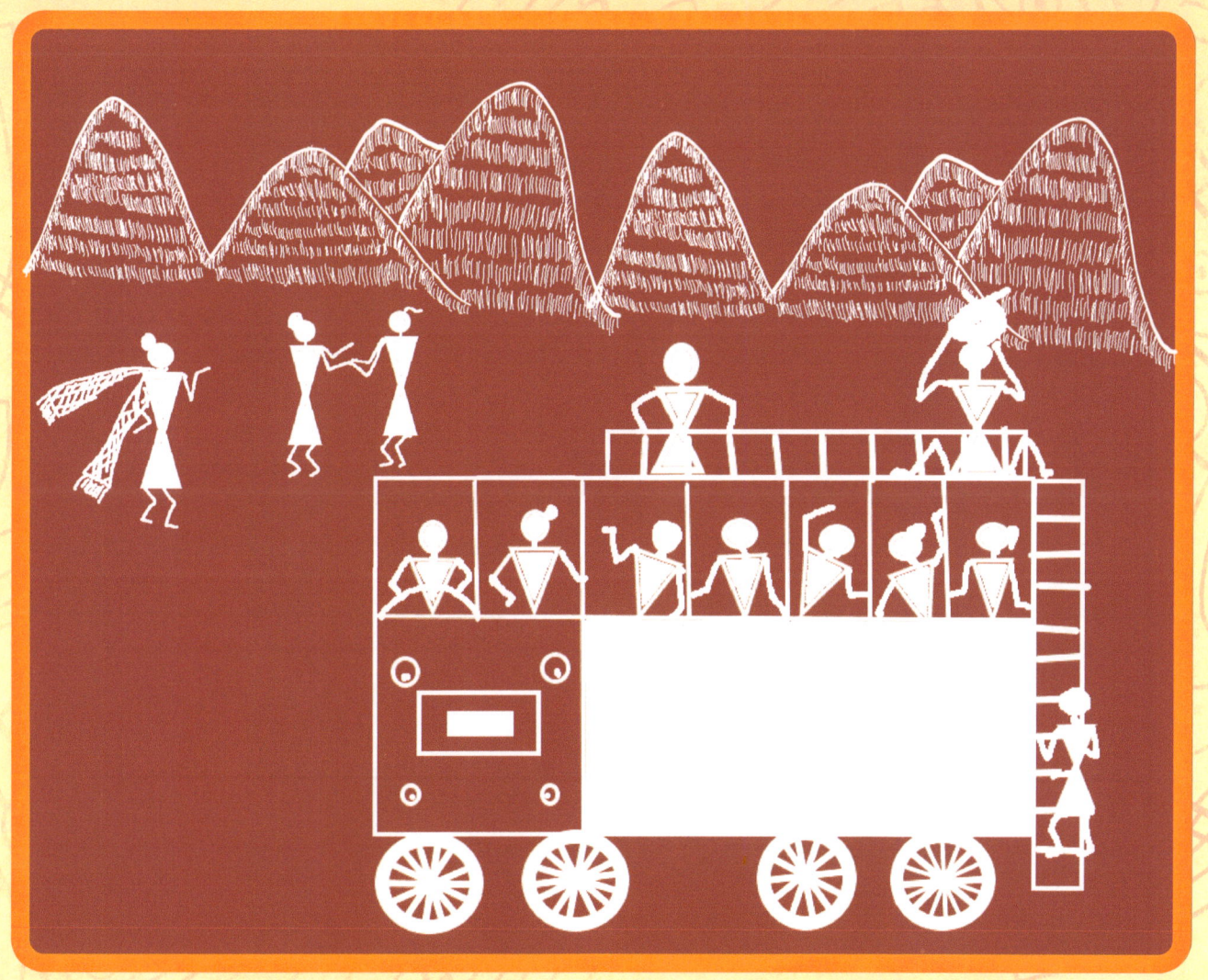

The **Buses** are crowded
most of the time
With people climbing on top
often sometimes

Warli art description

	Man
	Women
	Tarpa
	Drum
	Insect
	Bird

Warli art description

	Sun
	Moon
	Trees
	Bon fire
	Hut
	Dancing in circle

Match the following

   Man climbing tree

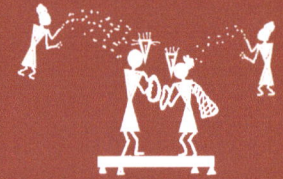   Eating together

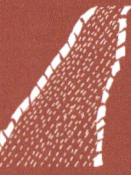   Fishing

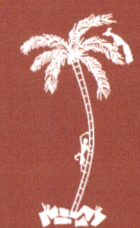   River

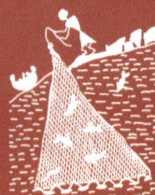   Wedding

About Author:

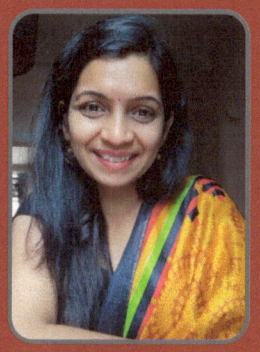

Namitha Tantri is a Poet, Author and Artist. She is a mother of two boys, an Indian living in Belgium. After working as a freelance writer, she started a creative writing blog and developed an interest in poetry. Her poetries are related to the reality of life, emotions, and positivity.

She has been a constant admirer of Warli art of India and is fascinated with the simplicity of warli art to narrate a story. Hence she uses Warli art for illustration in her books. Apart from poetries and art, she also creates useful planners to improve productivity and manage important tasks. Connect with Namitha Tantri on www.namithatantri.com

Other Warli related books by Namitha Tantri:

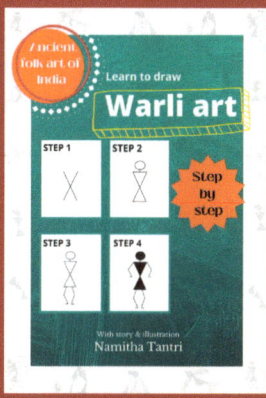

Learn to draw Warli art
(English edition)
ebook/paperback

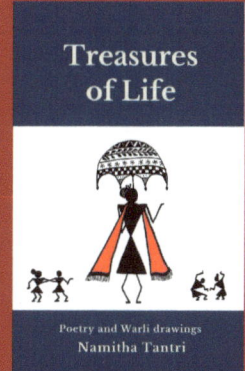

Treasures of life
Poetry with Warli art
(English edition)
ebook/paperback

www.namithatantri.com

www.ingramcontent.com/pod-product-compliance
Lightning Source LLC
Chambersburg PA
CBHW051835210526
45473CB00005B/1883